The Youngest Giraffe

Story by Elizabeth Russell-Arnot   Illustrations by Julian Bruère

The youngest giraffe had been running and playing all morning.

He was hot and thirsty
and he wanted to have a drink.

He looked around for his mother.
He could see her
walking down to the waterhole.

The other giraffes were thirsty, too.
They were all going down
to the waterhole.

The youngest giraffe
ran along beside them.

The giraffes looked around carefully
for lions.
They could see some zebras
drinking at the waterhole.
But today there were no lions
to be seen.
It was safe for the giraffes
to stand and drink near the zebras.

The youngest giraffe
wanted to be like the big giraffes
and the zebras.

He wanted to drink
from the waterhole.
He had never done this before.

The youngest giraffe
moved his legs out wide.

He put his neck down,
and he put his head down.
But he could not get
his mouth into the water.

He was very thirsty.

The youngest giraffe tried again.
He moved his legs out
just a little bit more.

He put his neck down,
and he put his head down.
But he **still** could not get
his mouth into the water.

The youngest giraffe
tried one more time.
He pushed his legs out
as wide as they would go.

And this time,
when he put his head down,
his mouth went
right into the water.

At last the youngest giraffe
could drink at the waterhole,
just like the others.

And so he drank and drank
until he was not thirsty any more.